Soil by Catherine Swire

ISBN 978-0-9926035-9-5

copyright © 2021 Catherine Swire
illustrations copyright © 2020 Marina Kolchanova

The author wishes to assert her moral and intellectual rights in relation to this work.

First printed 2021
02

ACKNOWLEDGEMENTS

The extract from *Mothers in Mourning* by Nicole Loraux translated by Corinne Pache is reproduced by the kind permissions of Cornell University Press and Georges Borchardt, Inc.

The publisher wishes to thank Marina Kolchanova for her generous permission to reproduce the illustrations in this book.

Cover photograph by the publisher.

Printed in the UK by Imprint Academic Ltd.

Published by The Artel Press
www.theartelpress.co.uk

"the Unforgetful has always been the Forgotten"
Nicole Loraux, Mothers in Mourning

Contents

for Mary who showed me the field

and Helen who taught me to turn the soil...

Soil: a Manifesto

or TRAUMA'S RELICS

Towards slow meaning

These poems explore the way trauma is inscribed in, and changed by,
landscape. Specifically, they look at distinct sites and monuments along
the Worcestershire - Herefordshire border. Each is imagined with a walk,
accompanied by a sketched map and prose; the words initiate movement and
are themselves a kind of work. To take these walks is to be slowly struck by
the visual connection between the discrete sites and through that to gain a
growing sense of a continuous landscape.

These embedded sites are chosen to arouse a reader's curiosity and to deepen
awareness of England's changing history from the ground up. As far as
possible, the poems let the places themselves speak. For all its limits, they
work with the idea that land, the ground itself, has a voice that requires an
immanent kind of listening - one focused on expressive experience and
on the semantic as well as geographic plain we share. They are intended
as susurrations from the landscape, an accompaniment to it, rather than a
pressure beyond it. In this way they come close to the quietness of loss, the
terrifying emptiness when 'violence's dream geometry' is allowed form in the
changing space of home.

The poems are also concerned with the shapes that trauma leaves in the
mind; the way it changes how we listen and respond. From the inside out,
they look at how violent loss can take away speech and the ability to read
and process meaning - in my own experience, that grew into a fascination

with the marks we make and the spectres that appear at the borderline of language, and the edge of literacy, and how they can connect the world.

Here, in this collection of eight poems, these shapes are traced. For example, in the re-visiting of the artificial or technological ear in *The Listening Station*. The building has become a symbol not only of expertise but also of the experience of deafness. In the treading of the infinity shape over circular palimpsests in *Caractacus in Flames*. In the artificial stone 'I' of *Obelisk*. In the glazier lifting death's toxic materials to make his slow-flowing art in *The Maker*. Finally, in the struggle between books and living beauty in *The Chained Library*. Worcestershire's ploughed earth and 'golden groves' have shaped affective landscapes and visions of the difficult change that is poetry's concern, from Langland to Geoffrey Hill.

However, their primary interest is in the way that traumatic response changes through human connection with the landscape. In one sense, in these poems, a vanishing. The Listening Station seems an overgrown cave, the obelisk appears as an idealised pencil sketch, the battle field is green grazing. But also a moving towards wholeness, a self quietness that accommodates the whole environment; in living terms, quite the opposite of disappearance, an assertion of connection; the clogged bell is revealed, the dingy cave re-scrutinised.

This work also connects with other writers and artists who engage with the complexity of raising remembrance of violent trauma through landscape, for example Anselm Kiefer, and poets who have approached aspects of radical trauma from the outside in, such as Simon Armitage and Owen Sheers. The landscapes represented are not pastoral or wild nor do they romantically express a pathetic fallacy. They show rather the land's expressive agency, through our physical engagement with it.

These poems are meant to be read aloud, preferably with images of the places and prior to a walk; several are written in a kind of dialogue between land and foot, artist and the one who suffers; a basic stepping, that in its acknowledgement of eclipse and silence, tries to make space for voice - and its annihilation. An act of forgetting in the deepest, most careful sense used by Toni Morrison or Nicole Loraux.

The scrutiny of trauma's marks extends outwards to look at the physical remains of political trauma. The cycle began before the coronavirus pandemic that muffled mouths all over the place. After a great deal of paralysing debate (repeatedly described as a non-bloody Civil War) Worcestershire, like England, voted to leave the European Union; a decision that is likely to have a longer term impact on our future than pandemic. The poems explore the other, extremely bloody, seventeenth century English Civil War that found partial resolution here, at Powick Bridge and in the Battle of Worcester.

Clearly, the complexity and profundity, the dialogue, of our relationship to Europe is particularly evident in this small county. On British Camp, where legendarily the Ancient Britons made their last flaming stand against Rome, lionised to nationalist song by Elgar in Caractacus. Through the violent club marks of Reformation in the cathedral, following schism from Rome, to the Second World War listening station. This current break with Europe, is not an end, but part of an ongoing interrogation of our relational geography, in which Great Britain, that originally took its name as a translation from a smaller part of France, Big Brittany, works again to remake its past.

Finally, the poems explore the assimilation of literary trauma in the way we make poems now. In this century in Europe, poetry continues to emerge from both modernism and its more playful child, postmodernism, with their emphases on fractured identity and mourning, the legacy of the violence of colonial domination and World War. A concern for wholeness, connectivity, the centrality of the environment, female and marginal voices, emerges in a digital age where poetry's verbal smallness, lightness (in every sense) works well on screen. However, the traces of modernist poetry are everywhere; both in free, impassioned, confessional verse - the absolute mode of our time - and in the evolution of our understanding of presence, mechanical making and landscape. In an age of dominant personalisation, self affirmation and affect, there is still scope to borrow modernism's insistence on models that are depersonalised and veiled. This is not to repress, but to hold pain at a distance and allow a border for what is un-reciprocal and speechless; the fact that lived suffering is most often not performance, but its absence. These poems, in that sense, work against sensational, instantaneous meaning and un-nuanced positivism in all its ecstatic, consumable seduction and dramatic emotion - preferring the slow accrual of sense. Slow meaning, bigger named after smaller and elsewhere, like our country. They acknowledge modernism, the mixing of speech patterns, old forms and female voices, moving through its twentieth century fixation on mourning, to observe landscape, continuity, resistance and presence.

It is upside down to end a manifesto with a beginning. The first working titles were Stupa, Reliquary, or Trauma's Relics, to reflect on Buddhist *stupas* - windowless, sturdy, stone, elongated domes built over the bones of saints or other relics - and the state of *stupor*. The dislocation of meaning between the site and the state and the repetition of sound, in chant and bell, felt central to the impact of trauma. Both in terms of the mental smoke, disassociation or stupor it causes, and how that trance of radical loss can be an in-between space of affirmative change.

However *Soil* in the end, seemed closer to the work of the poems themselves. Firstly, it holds the sense of contamination and waste in revisiting trauma and death. Secondly, it marks the sacred act of burial, the scattering of earth over a body from our most ancient cultures (for Antigone, for example, a fatal act of defiance in a regime that tyrannically refuses it). Thirdly, soil is the fundamental subject of the poems; the make up of the physical landscape of part of England now - its grime and growth.

Warm thanks to the artists and friends who have worked with me on a project which often felt vanished and valueless; that carried some of the dangerous energy of the damage it seeks to capture. In particular, Bridget Macdonald,whose good sense helped this book to grow and whose own quietly exquisite landscapes, here and of the mind, take my breath away. Also to Marina Kolchanova, whose maps' sensitivity to colour, innovative perspective - and fun - brighten and address from outside this fragmented region, reminding us the other is our map. They help to lift ground from where it is embedded in richer more playful ways, and to share the beautiful complexity of real, affective, landscape now.

Catherine Swire
Malvern, 2021

From Malvern

Guarlford Rd

Green
Dragon

Salt Path

Wood St

St Mary's Church

Grange Farm

Radio Listening Station

Woodbridge Farm

Rectory Ln

1. Guarlford

Guarlford

The first site to explore the integration of trauma in landscape through time is the derelict, brick-built listening station at Guarlford.

Here, during the Second World War, allied decoders discovered that Axis researchers were working to create V2 rockets; their work led to the destruction of the testing sites at Peenemunde. Afterwards, the listening station; blank, white-wired inside, compact and strong in scarlet brick, concrete and aluminium, bristling with masts and surrounded by barbed wire, slowly decayed; was reused as temporary housing by the local community. This poem looks in particular at the way that senses are exaggerated and seem separated from the body after sudden trauma or violence - the ear is replicated by super equipped radio surveillance, that signal in fact the opposite - the absence of living hearing, deafness. The function of the ear has been translated into technological apparatus.

The poem seeks a shape for that experience of alienation and return, the way that sudden trauma can displace our relationship to reality and meaning, at the level of communication. To do so, it combines a founding myth of Western philosophy, Plato's cave and the space outside it of perfect form, with a very ordinary, afternoon incident. A mother and daughter on a walk, bring along Philosophy notes to revise for a school test on a damp day. According to Plato, a world of perfect form exists outside everyday human experience within the cave of the world - which is merely a projection of shadows thrown up by a fire that burns behind those inside. The philosopher, like the one wrenched by sudden death, must step outside the cave (taking leave of human senses, including hearing) to witness formal perfection and sunlight, then make their difficult and seemingly doomed return to the cave of shadows to communicate the impossible vision.

In this poem, the World War II Listening Station that the mother and daughter discover, provides an ideal but separated model of elite understanding in crisis, a perfected style of listening, bristling with technology, but empty of sentience. Through time, it has become integrated with the natural landscape, marked by physical dilapidation. It appears in its emptiness and symbolism, to embody a cave, or the living world itself. In this story, the mother and daughter, by getting off the road, despite local warnings, explore the past together and find voice and shape for a complex experience of return from the un-hearable.

Listening Station

In-between day - pale grey mud - wet winter-bleached
grass, all long, lolled over what was green -
sodden stile, bald band of water -

Don't cross over there! A dog woman calls, *It's full of dung!*
Half listening, taking in her collie's pearl blind eye,
my daughter ambles up, Timberlands a-gape, gripping
Revision Flash Cards of green biro facts -
Plato's cave - where shadow meets form.
Why follow the deaf dog on autopilot home?

Climb. Leap. Wade. Through faded, flooded grass, back
to the Listening Station. Concrete lintels and rust frames
high round the arcs of bramble leaves, December
bruised, blackened, red, green, yellow, septic tank choked
coal house, peer through window blanks - at nothing?

Even Guarlford's landscape holds up the event.
A common field cut out. Blank, brick walls. White cube inside.
Cordoned guns. Barbed coils. The unidentified forbidden.
Lattice towers. Click dials. Generator. Elite
netting of slow, deathly code, condensed
to name some harm abroad, this time V2 and Peenemunde.

The air, discharged of answers, sifts its own light. After boffins
Vi and Ernie. Twelve cows. Squatters from The Close...
My daughter's crossed the roadside hedgerow now -
she calls to me - fumbling with quiet ears for history
and the day. Between us, the Listening Station's
a wishy wash of dying colours, everything.
Windows out, dark spot. Wild, choked up cave.

2. Worcester

Worcester

The next two poems take a different approach to trauma and silence, through two of the biggest smashes of modern British History; the Reformation and the Civil War.

Both concern the destructive, creative gap of separation sudden death opens up, here between parent and child. The former between father and son. The second between mother and daughter. Significantly the first, about Worcester Cathedral and Henry and Arthur, father and son, describes a building; the latter about Powick Bridge and the meeting point of two rivers, mother and daughter, describes the commingling, transparent water crash between the Teme and the Severn.

Chantry Song is an imagined sonnet in Worcester Cathedral whispered over the grave of Prince Arthur, Henry VII's first born son. Arthur died aged fifteen at Ludlow Castle, his grave lies within a highly carved chantry near the altar that was defaced in the Reformation; the stone saints within it have had their faces beaten off. Carved in Purbeck marble, the chantry has the yellowing, honed, highly carved feel of ivory. The ivory gate also refers to the route through which Aeneas escapes the underworld in the Aeneid; the gate of false dreams. Aeneas, paradoxically, enters the world of the dead through the horn gate of true dreams. So the sonnet moves from absence of feeling, through a focus on the black box that holds Arthur, to a connection with the whole building. The reign of Henry VIII remains a national focus, whether in school history syllabus, prize winning novel, or West End musical. Its definitive violence of which the break with European power in Rome was only a part, followed the unforeseen, untimely loss of the one who was meant to rule. Sudden family change because of the death of Prince Arthur, marked by a chantry the size of a caravan in a provincial cathedral, was a small but critical factor in the political wrenching of England, the legacy of which we still inhabit.

Three voices are bound together in one exasperated love sonnet. An uncomfortable break between the first four lines of careful mourning, the wrenched voice of Henry, which seems to exemplify radical change but in fact reifies and responds to parental fixity within the poetic form, and the final quatrain willing an opening to the greater, beautiful building.

Chantry Song

Along the red tile vein of the cathedral,

a little room of bleached ribs - of stone lace - holds our First Born

gone. Click through the ivory gate. Who, from the dapple horn,

can act where faces blur the bone incense puff of his potential?

you -

    who...

wrecks the Kingdom, snubs the pope,

calls wife, *sister, bitch-witch, traitor, slag*

breaks things and gets fat, mashes hope

out on saints' faces with the crow bars of my thugs!

Reformation?

        Sure! Back I'll bash you

To that cut black box! *Great parents! Hell, yes! Arthur too.*

O calcified lace! Brain hacked bruiser! Ossified loss!

Gate of false dreams! England, arguing the toss

with Europe. The heart - an empty rib room - while

the whole, living cathedral vaults up - in exile!

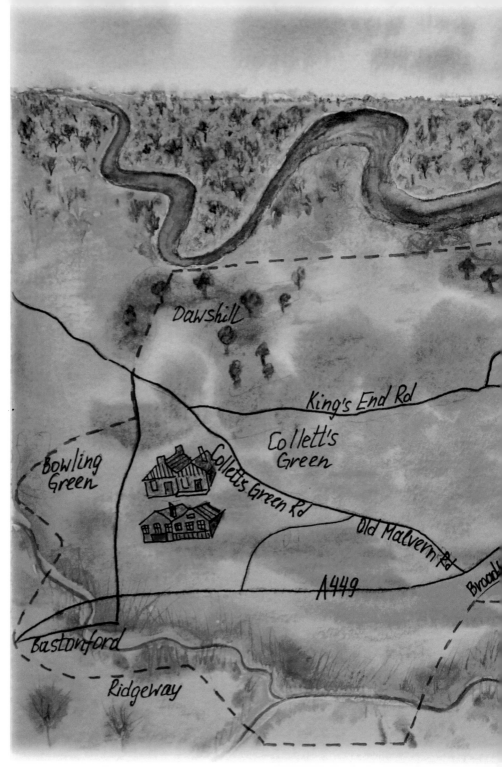

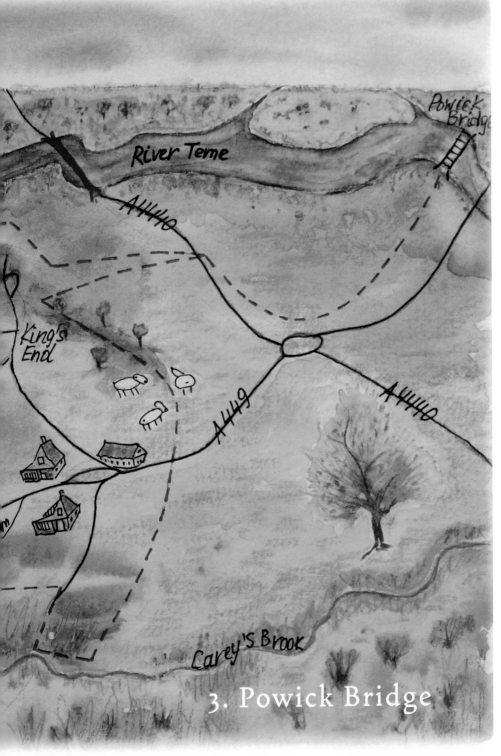

River Teme

Powick Bridge

A4440

King's End

A449

A4440

Carey's Brook

3. Powick Bridge

Powick Bridge

Worcester not only represents the violence of the Reformation, it is the site of two critical battles in the Civil War. The Battle of Powick Bridge, a Royalist victory, and the Battle of Worcester, a Parliamentarian one that resulted in the flight of the king.

This latter took place in sites all over the city but critically at the juncture of the Teme and the Severn, where the two rivers smash into each other. The Parliamentarians won here by making their own temporary pontoon bridges from upturned boats. In contrast, Powick Bridge, beautiful and ancient, made of small pink and white bricks with iron stapled capstones and parapet 'refuges' for mounted horses to allow wagons to pass, held for the Royalists in a skirmish. The area around the rivers, and at Powick particularly, is cyclically devastated by floods that leave a stinking, bile-like fertile mud and debris every winter. Broken sticks like strewn nests are scattered everywhere. The battlefield site at Powick, marked by a panel with a reproduced oil painting of battle, is striking in its quietness. A raised green field above the flood bric-a-brac holds two mounds, each with a man-made opening onto water, in contrast to the wilder flood plain on the other side of the river.

This poem was written at New Year, when severe floods blocked most paths in the area. It considers other hidden Civil Wars, for example clashes and bonds between mothers and daughters, under-explored because of their fluidity, seemingly transparent, like the water that represents them here. Nevertheless this invisible, unacknowledged drama, this transparent civil war between monolithic and democratic power on the shared territory of the body, expresses the central energy of many lives. Like the Civil War itself, in some ways, such clashes cannot have the clarity of a single resolution. A battle rather, literally and metaphorically, about currency and bridge.

Once again the landscape from Powick Bridge and along the river up to Worcester seems to reveal dispassionately the most vital energies of combat in a way the political conflict (that killed a far larger proportion of the English and Scottish population even than twentieth century world war) no longer can.

Powick Bridge, New Year's Day

Flood's a mother fed up with her children!
She's thrown everything out of their room;
Discarded their sacred - black-yellow football -
Cracked up lunch box - so many broken trees!

Flood's suicidal she's swallowed dimension!
Each grass gun-grey, each dead leaf mud-matt
Slaphappy rejection, a reclaymation,
Each blade bleached by her - each bug bile fat!

Flood's stony broke she's blowing her currency!
Making a land great only for dogs - dogs who splash
Spatter and bite for the smash of it...
Reject her monotone light. The scraped burn of her banks.

*

Notes

Bridges made in battle don't survive -

    Straddle-boats lashed in a turtle huddle –
    drum, drum, drum - drones defend the hive –
    soldiers' standard-shoes stamp up three waters –
    tip up, trade, split, splice, segment – our mother is alive –

Plain platforms of passage can survive -

    Such pretty clarity! Frosted coral bricks zig out for horse and cattle -
    a grown man parks his Mum by 'History! Do Not Drive!'
    father and son (on bikes) read a printed battle panel -

O daughter! Water under bridge, all our found ground, survive. -

Field's the body risen above her smuttings...
critical battle in our Civil War -
winner - loser - (almost) exchangeable... the king
drops away like a spider on an invisible skein -

So lovely, her green, as if Spring itself re-mothered her -
who will remember the dusk struggle here? Two mounds,
Two monuments. A manhole draining mould water,
a zinc tank containing pure water, we cannot

be sure what counts most in our own history
- in this time of 'non violent Civil War' -
where Teme crashes with Severn,
truth a watermark and a silver line.

4. Sugar Loaf

Sugar Loaf, Obelisk Walk

On the walk over Sugar Loaf Hill above Great Malvern, looking across Herefordshire to the horizon of the Eastnor deer park, a stone obelisk echoes and challenges the spikes of the trees.

The obelisk is a sign of mourning for three members of the Somers Cocks family. Alongside a record of distinguished and eloquent loss in the Peninsular Wars, a brief piece remembers a son lost in France in 1759 as an idealistic teenager, "possessed of an ample patrimony, he preferred honour to security". The parental tone of despair, pride and exasperation in the inscription is movingly reinforced by the scarcity of words and blank stone, compared to the stately, long crafted sentences on the other sides. Also by the frailty, artificiality and persistence of the single I on the landscape made by the obelisk needle from many directions. In the hazy light common at the top of Sugar Loaf, looking out over Herefordshire, the horizon can seem to blur into a single profile pattern; trees, obelisk, hill. Almost like an idealised, received image from China 'The Orient', for example in willow pattern; or the way figures in Japanese woodblock printed books merge seamlessly in a device of woven fabrics and nature that together compose the picture. But of course there is a shadow as well as a pleasure in holding so much coding, as the word Orient, with its glib fantasies of the East shows. The view is full of other fictions, of Tolkien's Shire opposed to the stench of Mordor; Tolkien used to drink at The Unicorn pub at the bottom of the hill. The land has echoes of Narnia folded above the town of gas lamps where Lewis was teaching (they were friends). The blue blur of the tree-softened, hop-striped hills, in such marked contrast to the wide Severn plain, seems like a Renaissance Italian portrait backdrop. How to keep walking and open to living weather surrounded by so much predetermined meaning? The answer a dog.

This poem which explores the dreamed or coded identity, the artifice of the separated I of mourning, is about flow and has very little punctuation, its only capitals show real and imaginary place.

The first walk is to the view of the Obelisk from Sugar Loaf, the second a direct walk to the Obelisk itself through the deer park.

Obelisk

the person who was coming with me didn't
in the end because of a fall so in the end
it was just me and the dog

the children heads down flaked in
snow scribble of mock-mock exams that never happened
by the time I got out of the house people

were almost down with their dogs blown inside
out like umbrellas our dog's head down
back fur a-burnish wind-burrowing and

both of us wanted it over when we turned
into the direct westward aspect
of Eastnor and the obelisk

*

the obelisk like a light pencil sketch on the horizon among the

natural flow of growing mounds an upright pencil on the sea

of white mist, the milk lake over Wales...or the Orient

so that for one moment I thought how trauma sudden loss

can re-present what once seemed natural as if it has been drawn and

how it raises a single artificial I within both worlds

a mark of concrete difference -

not a tree it will not grow but part like them of the horizon -

that's what I thought til the dog scattered a billowing

white one - he's friendly I called - lost again in the wind

5. British Camp

British Camp

British Camp, in a myth refuted by Tacitus, is the site where Ancient Britons led by Caractacus took a last stand against the Romans.

From the top of one of the two saddled hills or on the spur it is shockingly simple to imagine a Roman legion approaching in a line of brass helmets across the plain. The poem traces the shape of infinity, the figure of eight, which in its looped circles, seems to mark survival, editing and prohibiting speech, after trauma. British Camp is still dug into the shape of ancient defences; a concentric bind of ruts, dug by antler horns where, apparently, horses and trees (both symbols of childhood and continuity) were burned up, to hold off the invasion. The poem has the dreamlike, enfolded, quality of the manmade lines on the hills themselves, and says something uneasily circular about trauma's visions of infinity and the way it seems to hold up space within time.

Ultrasound scan and spectral imaging show that in British Camp, the infinity shaped ditch marks surround the burned up circle shapes of torched huts, without disrupting the peaceful surface. Again through these technologies of blind seeing, the return to Plato's cave, these rings emerge like a hundred black zeros, although they are lost to the naked eye. So it can feel that the hills hold within them a kind of occluded language; pure, almost mathematical shapes created by the event with flames. The patriotically critical myth of defiance was made by Elgar into a fay, nationalistic opera, full of startling arias, druids, oak garlands and wode. Here, Caractacus the hero in flames connects with the Germanic Siegfried in Kiefer's paintings, the boy on the burning deck and Orfeus.

The poem seeks to explore the impossible mythic space which has so affected recent English politics and Britain's 'original' island identity. Here, Caractacus sings with flame as what he loves vanishes. All nationalistic dreams are founded and defined by the connections that they exclude and nowhere is that clearer than the story of Caractacus himself, who according to historians, enchanted the Romans after his capture with the fluency of his speech and travelled to Rome, not as chained prisoner but guest. He stayed on in the great capital, Rome's Refugee, because he liked the lifestyle and his villa, with apricots and central heating, there. Reportedly he asked Caesar why on earth the Romans, with such a good life at home, wanted to take Britain in the first place.

This poem however places Caractacus in the moment of kingship and annihilation, the foundation of dream shape...

Caractacus in Flames

- this hill holds the shape of silence -
absence grooves the slopes - lets shadows grieve -

figure of eight - shelf of curves - circumflex
dis/proves the loss of tongue - its tilde and breve -

*

voiceless/ traced - dissolving ground -
the mourning body couples with its shape -

pointless hour - by necessary hour -
confronting/back to find/losses' landscape -

*

radiating grass - sunlessness emits -
zero by zero - a hundred burned out huts -

palimpsest rings under ruched grass stirrups -
homes on fire - horses, trees blazing in ruts -

*

a momentary hero - Caractacus in flames -
blooming orange oil, Orfeus on top -

death's the Legion line moving on the plain -
life the curve of earth that will not stop

*

blown from his course like tourists or grass -
this silent silo - holds/absorbs - effaces/sets free —

at night it shapes our sleep - symbol of survival -
sound's erasure - violence's dream geometry.

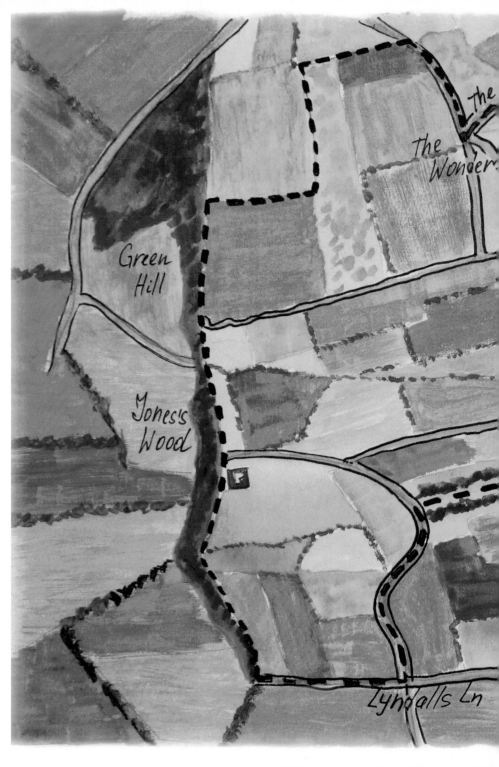

Green Hill

Jones's Wood

The Wonder.

Lyndalls Ln

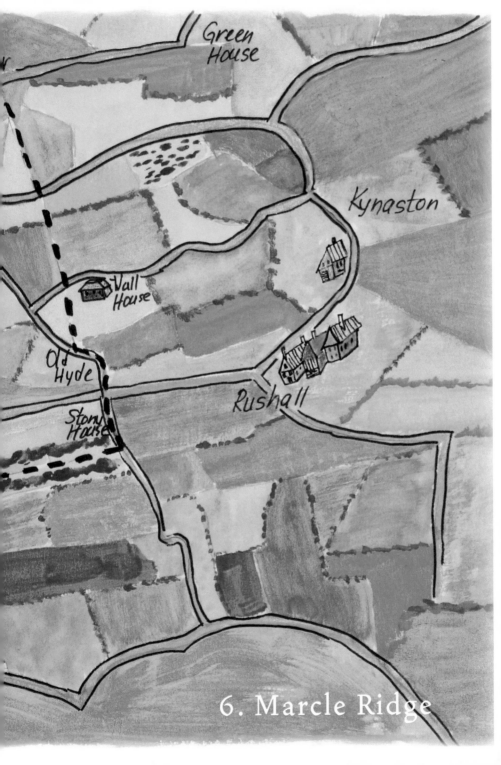

Green
House

Kynaston

Wall
House

Old
Hyde

Rushall

Stony
House

6. Marcle Ridge

The Wonder, Marcle Ridge

This poem slows down and flattens, weaves, the effect of trauma on a sense of home; the collapse to a sense of belonging that violent loss can trigger.

It also explores the more general need culturally to possess and represent (in some senses to purloin) that experience; recalling the debate around statues of slave owners in Oxford and Cambridge and the way those who know their lives are still blighted by the legacy of slavery might feel witnessing that. The subject is the 1588 Sheldon Tapestry Map of Worcestershire, hanging in the hall of Weston Library in the New Bodleian, Oxford. The tapestry is itself one of four woven maps of the Midlands; one of which is scattered as fragments. It represents a large number of Worcestershire/Herefordshire villages and amongst many small familiar places, an unheard of village, Worlde's End. Although the library curator in Oxford was mystified by Worlde's End, locally it was relatively easy to discover the incident the name marked. This event of 1575 rocked England and is still remembered around Much Marcle, Rushall, Woolhope and Kynaston as 'The Wonder'. A hill began to move and collapse in on itself in a kind of inland tsunami, roaring for three days, so that preachers claimed it as a sign of apocalypse. The landslide remade the landscape, in permanent, slumped soil ripples, destroying a church and livestock. This event like every disaster - often fairly - was claimed as the result of human wrongdoing - the village at its centre was renamed Worlde's End. The place where the soil slid is still very visible in grassy folds. It is now deserted, strange-shaped countryside; but would have been teeming in the sixteenth century, when agriculture and this area itself, as the Oxford tapestry map shows, were central to the British economy.

The Wonder site's almost comic current blankness, says something profound and often overlooked about the site of trauma, in the context of its immediate fascination. That is, how groping back to life often re-inscribes 'normality' as quieter and more bland, in contrast to the lives of those fascinated around Auden's 'drawing down of blinds'.

In the poem, rhymes begin to fall down the stanzas like the earth, the whole sewn in clumsy, black stitched pictures like the tapestry, while the bell notes intone. Herefordshire and Worcestershire themselves have a long history of named, sacred bells and Ledbury, Much Marcle's nearest town, has recently become the first town in the world to cast a commemoration bell to mark the suffering of Covid 19.

Around 1840, the earth on the ridge itself gave up the bell that had been buried in the field chapel that fell; the moment's buried sound. The bell was hung in a local house. The parochial peace of this conclusion, behind closed curtains, seemed to chime with the comfortably woven tapestry and the general ignorance about the extraordinary tale of the vanished village. So in the poem, the profound, unassimilable, is stitched up into a jaunty rhyming foot note. The power of the image of the resurrected bell, plays with the wider resonance of the image worldwide, perhaps most powerfully in Tarkovsky's film Andrei Rublev, a vision where the remaking of a bell becomes the symbol of personal, artistic and national regeneration.

Aperiatur Terra - Oxford

Slubbed with chubby pears and marrows slap
bang in Bodley's entrance! Worcestershire - where
we're from - sewn up in a map.

Look where we live now! (A finger moving on the wall)
down through familiar villages towards 'Worldes End'.
'Which was driven down by the removing of the ground'

Black silken words. But like a place...So strange!
The cartographic expert shrugs, "No one can recall..."
What! Not recall your tapestry holds in apocalypse?

So I come home and follow faded threads
of chat 'three days' 'deceitful ground' 'horrible roar'
'hole' 'permanently higher' 'land fall'

*

Note

a plough struck up a buried bell showing
in lead and clotted earth how sudden violence -
that stops the tongue and makes home's name a sentence -
can yield in earth through time; that parting and growing –
while horror lies in many soft hands sewing
the bell, that's lost, lies in the soil's hoeing

We drive then. Past a pub sign, *The Slip* -
A man hands up running, land melting behind,
on our minds the earth itself, its humus, grain by grain

crumbling like air when you wake up at night, gagging
at black seams, the foaming flowing grass splits its lip
spits out the fence, the chapel tilts and falls -

sheep with gaping mouths struggle to right
themselves til the earth gulps them - who can resist
terror as a sign? Not priests who took up England in their grip,

suddenly clear about themselves, the world's end, sin
as the unnatural, strange land sunk - literally abject -
still so quiet here you feel you're falling....

*

Return - the Sheldon map has lost its woolly bloom.
The yellow of the cloth under the glaze might be flayed skin.
The pink threads 'dyed and mordant' stain the room.

Upper Wel...

Mayall's Farm

A4104

Black Hill

Wood
Farm

Days
Farm

Marl Bank

Vew Tree
Farm

Marlbank
Farm

Ground's
Farm

Elliot's
Farm

Welland
Farm

7. Malvern

Little Malvern Priory

This poem imagines Master Glazier, Richard Twigge, who worked on stained glass windows around Malvern in the fifteenth century, making death's tracks into art.

Details of medieval lead making are described in Theophilus Presbyter and the poem was prompted by the extraordinary leaded glass portraits in Little Malvern Priory. This small church, and former Benedictine monastery, holds the only living portrait of the elder Prince-in-the-Tower, Edward V. In glass, across a blank pane from his father and his mother, the image is much shattered and blanked by weather and the Civil War. Edward's mother, Elizabeth Woodville, and his father, Edward IV are also represented here with their two daughters, Catherine and Bridget. Elizabeth took sanctuary with all four of her children, when her husband Edward IV died, but was persuaded to hand over her two sons - supposedly to care - in fact to their death. The mystery of how the twelve year old Edward and his younger brother died, and the suspicion they were murdered, has inspired novels, plays and a high court trial. Our current queen and parliament maintain the secret; refusing permission to use new technologies to identify potential skeletons.

In this examination of the effects of trauma, however, the art of glass-making, anticipates the death that it represents. The paintings were made during the princes' life time and put up around the time of their murder. At the simplest level the glass images in the window are mimetic of the paralysis of sudden loss, the way that it seems to freeze and denature identity, time and emotional bond. Time bulges and appears to stop within the lead window. The image of the prince himself projects an older and more powerful figure than he ever became - in contrast the lead work of the glazier offers a different time pattern, steady, linear and procedural. The poem has two voices. Lead, the toxic skin of water and death, pipes and coffins, is a strong part of medieval picture making - but unobserved as an essential part of its vision. The making of lead portraits connects with the seams of poetry. Here each stanza is literally linked by 'lead'. Although the church is almost unchanged since the Middle Ages with banners and animal carving, the churchyard is well maintained and current (including the grave of an auctioneer carved with a gavel and a medical student covered by an avalanche). The earth along the central footpaths to Little Malvern Priory, that was probably walked by the best, first English dream vision poet Langland, is often cracked, between the corn or cabbage, as if preparing for a quiet and natural resurrection.

The Maker

Lead calms hold up a mother gone -
a queen and - separately - her child.
The child's head and hands are white
sky-in-the-dark - sickening with power -
ghost trees of fine veins sip sap to
nothing - the Master Glazier's
brush stops in black lines
radioactive rays cannot reduce.

Rick Twygge (small part of a tree) pours a lead line

Lead cuts the lost boy's head off at the throat -
separates a mother from her eyes -
nets up sky into the father's face -
breaks the book in half and blurs it with a desk -
slices mother - son - a clear pane - lifts
a crown away - leaves a nun's head floating bodiless

beside a mother soldered to her daughters - traces
cities in the air - mangles an angel's face but not her trumpet -

Rick Twygge peels lead from chalk and pares it fine

Lead makes the pane The Tower - the suffering, display -
reframes the boy as see-through, seams him
as he dies - something spectacularly real,
young, gentle in those pale hands -
the halo of the book and of the mother's hair an
equal yellow - lead re-pens nature's vision
in death's alphabet — opens afterlife - poisons
the man-who-masters-art's-paid-up-technologies.

Rick Twygge loops one dark letter - one long h flange

Lead holds up liquid that's too slow for tears.
Musk dark, in this tiny church, a banner marks
Resurgam...two tiny wood pigs stuff themselves
on a carved arm. A wire donation bowl, biro rota
signature for flowers, tub of instant coffee.

And this pulse - to slip out salty from lead's complex eye

into the clicking corn and hike with a big dog

down crack-floor lines split by a pilgrim sun -

Rick Twygge solders up lead to meet rain, wind and change...

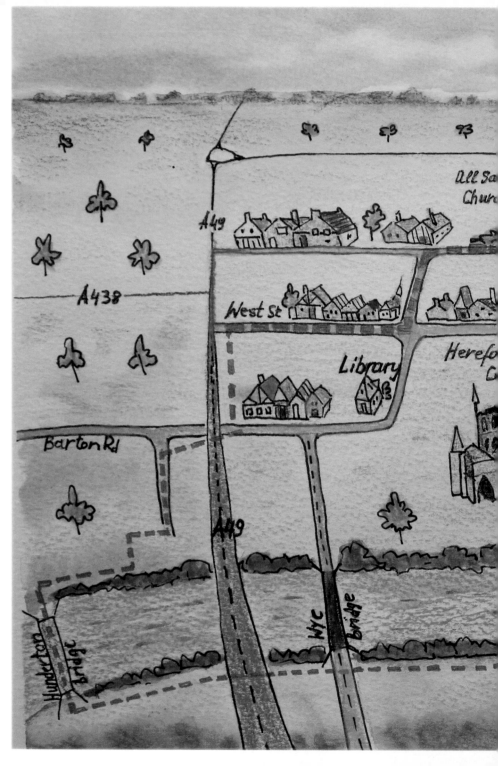

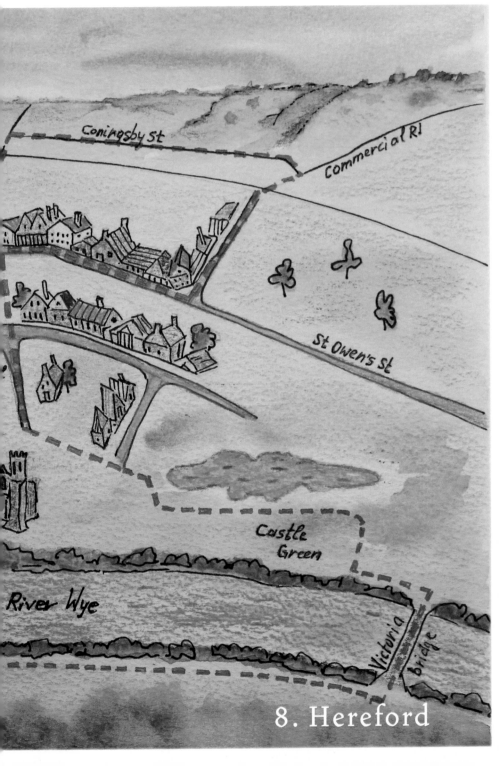

8. Hereford

Hereford

This final poem touches on the way trauma centrally can alienate from language - not only taking away natural speech but destroying the ability to read - accompanied by a sense of exile from knowledge.

Nowhere is the tension between the illiterate and the written word so clear as in the symbol of the chained library in Hereford where books are visibly shackled by a complex sliding iron lock, bar and chain system. They appear both intensely valuable and also like prisoners. The enchained books themselves are magnificent calligraphic works inside but appear shrivelled, old and brown on the shelves.

Ironically one of the largest books on the current library shelves in Hereford is a Wycliffite bible, a secret translation of the word of God into English crafted to release believers from confinement within the Latin of the church - a banned text at the time of the monastic libraries - and itself an angel moth of delivery in the guise of substantial conformity.

In a recent exhibition at the library, a prayer book on display showed parts of Thomas Beckett's liturgy scribbled out with black charcoal. Years after the saint's death, his witness posed a political threat to that Donald Trump of a king, Henry VIII, because he preferred Rome to English rule. The raw childish black scribble marks of the trauma-king over the exquisite, spiritually compliant transcribed script of the liturgy are very powerful alongside the chains.

Outside the library there is a beautiful walk through Bishop's Fields that feels a good place to end - a great patch of ginger, saffron and burgundy coloured trees, green space and black water - whose unstrained, living beauty and clear reflections lie in connective contrast to the library inside.

Returning to the Chained Library

Chains are pouring over books like water
veiling the cliff with mud and rain
like words half learned and thoughts
derivative covering the Word Before
flame inked that black bars restrain -

What does the rain say?

                    The rain says pour,

A guide lifts up a book and shows a manacle
'No book can be tethered by spine edge,'
she says, 'You have to feel - right to the lip -
the opening - so books sit in reverse -
these pages open on the ledge...'

What does the lip say?

                    The lip says pierce!

She points to a dingy flower-press of angel moths -
big oblong mushroom - dried out, gill by gill -
Wycliffe's bible! Secret text that unfixed
the bar - catalyst to twist Rome's words awry
onto dry tongues - here, too - chained like a mangy kestrel!

What does the moth say?

The moth says fly...

Behind her, open - trauma's book. The poetry of being vanishes.
Cancel the saints, Thomas! Scribble in death's trance
over the prior, beautifully made page.
Primal scrawl that cannot read or learn,
feeling's chapter cancelled sans performance.

What does the charcoal say?

The charcoal says burn.

The exhibition's over. In Bishop's Field, nature's too
original to be displaced. In the black, still pool
desire touches will, as roots touch their reflection.
The agency of absence - mourning - shifts its name
to loss on the lit surface - beneath the living branches
leaves are free and wave in talking flame.

X

The Artel Press
Liverpool, 2021